The New Novello Choral Edition

WOLFGANG AMADEUS MOZART

Coronation Mass
Mass in C (K.317)

for soprano, alto, tenor and bass soloists, SATB and orchestra

Revised by Michael Pilkington

Order No: NOV 072505

NOVELLO PUBLISHING LIMITED
14-15 Berners Street, London, W1T 3LJ

It is requested that on all concert notices and programmes acknowledgement is made to 'The New Novello Choral Edition'.

Es wird gebeten, auf sämtlichen Konzertankündigungen und Programmen 'The New Novello Choral Edition' als Quelle zu erwähnen.

Il est exigé que toutes notices et programmes de concerts, comportent des remerciements à 'The New Novello Choral Edition'.

Orchestral material is available on hire from the Publisher.

Orchestermaterial ist beim Verlag erhältlich.

Les partitions d'orchestre sont en location disponibles chez l'editeur.

Permission to reproduce from the Preface of this Edition must be obtained from the Publisher.

Die Erlaubnis, das Vorwort dieser Ausgabe oder Teile desselben zu reproduzieren, muß beim Verlag eingeholt werden.

Le droit de reproduction de ce document à partir de la préface doit être obtenu de l'éditeur.

Cover illustration: first page of the autograph score of Mozart's *Coronation Mass* (K.317) (courtesy of the Bibliotheka Jagiellońska, Cracow).

© Copyright 2000 Novello & Company Limited

Published in Great Britain by Novello Publishing Limited
Head office: 14-15 Berners Street, LONDON, W1T 3LJ
Tel +44 (0)20 7612 7400   Fax +44 (0)20 7612 7400

Exclusive Distributors:
Hal Leonard Europe Limited
42 Wigmore Street
Marylebone, London, W1U 2RY
Email: info@halleonardeurope.com

PREFACE

Mozart's *Mass in C*, K.317 was finished on 23 March 1779, and was probably written for the Archbishop of Salzburg for performance on Easter Sunday, April 4, of the same year. The first documented performance of the work is at the coronation of Francis I of Austria in August 1792, although it is possible that the work was performed at the coronation of Leopold II in 1791 in Prague. The connection with these two coronations earned the *Mass in C* the title by which it is best known, the *Coronation Mass*, distinguishing it from Mozart's seventeen other Mass settings, no less than seven of which are in the key of C.

There is some uncertainty regarding the horn parts of the *Coronation Mass*. They appear on separate sheets at the end of the autograph score, and were, in fact, separated from the score at some time, for they have their own page numbers and a note indicating that they belong to this Mass. There is no way of knowing whether Mozart intended to use horns from the beginning and had no room for them on the paper he used for the main body of the score, or whether he added them later. It appears that horns were seldom used at the cathedral (in Salzburg?), so that perhaps they can be considered optional extras.

The edition of this work that this revision replaces was edited by the founder of the Novello publishing house, Vincent Novello. The *Coronation Mass* was one of a number of masses by Mozart and Haydn that Vincent Novello published "at his own cost of time and money, in order to introduce them, in accessible form, among his countrymen in England"[1]. Novello provided an organ accompaniment tailored to the capabilities of the amateur organist, which was, to a large degree, a realisation of the figured bass with voice parts added, rather than a reduction from the orchestral score. This revised edition is based on Mozart's autograph, reproduced in facsimile in 1998 by the Internationale Stiftung Mozarteum Salzburg.

In the original score the solo and chorus voice parts share the same four staves because the solo singers would have been members of the choir. This explains the mixture of crotchets and quavers at the end of the soloists' phrase at bar 114 of the Credo. This revised edition has a new accompaniment derived from the orchestral score. A few slurs (with strokes) and dynamics (in square brackets) have been added. There is one actual alteration of Mozart's clear notation: in Bar 12 of the Kyrie the first note in the second violins (lower note of RH) is a b in the autograph. Although the same thing happens in the equivalent place at bar 61 of the Agnus Dei, this strong doubling of the major third and omission of the fifth of the chord is surely an oversight, and has here been changed to a *d*.

Michael Pilkington
Old Coulsdon 1999

---

1   Rosemary Hughes, 'Vincent Novello', article in *New Grove Dictionary of Music and Musicians*, ed. Stanley Sadie, London 1980.

MASS IN C

KYRIE

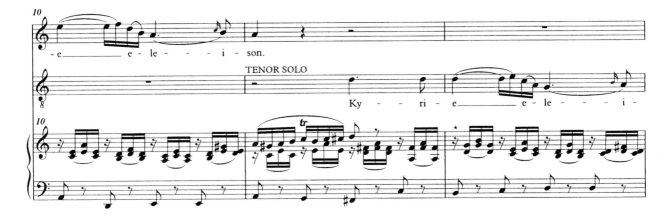

GLORIA

6

8

10

12

13

14

CREDO

Do - mi-num Je - sum Chris - tum, Fi - li - um De - i u - ni - ge - ni -

-tum. Et ex Pa - tre, ex Pa-tre na - tum an -

- te om - ni - a, om-ni-a sæ - - cu - la. De - um de

di — e, se - cun - dum, se - cun - dum Scrip - tu — - ras. Et as - cen —
di — e, se - cun - dum, se - cun - dum Scrip - tu — - ras. Et as - cen —
di — e, se - cun - dum, se - cun - dum Scrip - tu — - ras. As - cen —
di — e, se - cun - dum, se - cun - dum Scrip - tu — - ras. Et as - cen —

- - dit in cæ — - - lum:— se - det, se - det ad dex - te - ram
- dit in cæ — - lum: se - det, se - det ad
- dit in cæ — - lum: se - det, se - det ad dex - te - ram
- dit in cae — - lum: se - det, se - det ad dex - te - ram

Pa — tris, ad dex - te - ram Pa — - tris. Et
dex — te - ram, ad dex - te - ram Pa — - tris. Et
Pa — tris, ad dex - te - ram Pa — - tris. Et
Pa — tris, ad dex - te - ram Pa — - tris. Et

32

*see Preface

38

SANCTUS

Andante maestoso

*autograph has 'Osanna' throughout

42

BENEDICTUS

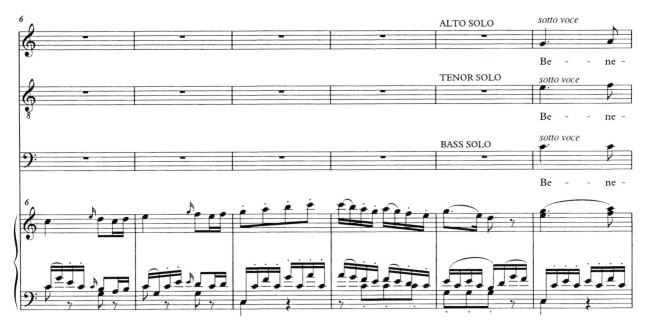

44

46

*autograph has 'Osanna' throughout

48

*autograph has 'Osanna' throughout

50

AGNUS DEI

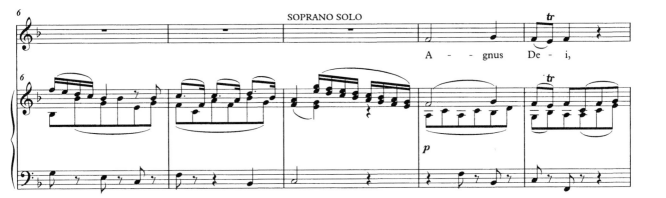

52

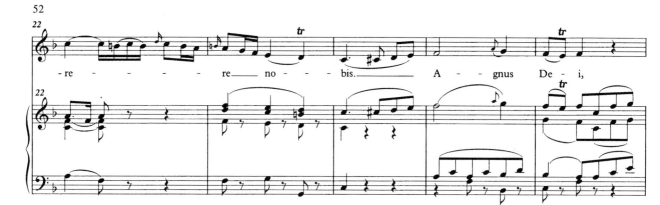

Andante con moto

*see Preface

54

56